GRAPHIC GREEK MYTHS AND LEGENDS

THE TWELVE LABORS OF HERCULES

By Nick Saunders
Consultant: Dr. Thorsten Opper, Curator of Greek
and Roman Antiquities, British Museum, London

WORLD ALMANAC® LIBRARY

YA-G
SAU

Please visit our web site at: www.garethstevens.com
For a free color catalog describing World Almanac® Library's list of high-quality books and multimedia programs, call 1-800-848-2928 (USA) or 1-800-387-3178 (Canada). World Almanac® Library's fax: (414) 332-3567.

Library of Congress Cataloging-in-Publication Data available upon request from publisher. Fax (414) 336-0157 for the attention of the Publishing Records Department.

ISBN-13: 978-0-8368-7751-9 (lib. bdg.)
ISBN-13: 978-0-8368-8151-6 (softcover)

This North America edition first published in 2007 by
World Almanac® Library
A Member of the WRC Media Family of Companies
330 West Olive Street, Suite 100
Milwaukee, WI 53212 USA

Illustrators: Bookmatrix

World Almanac® Library managing editor: Valerie J. Weber
World Almanac® Library art direction: Tammy West

Printed in Canada

1 2 3 4 5 6 7 8 9 10 10 09 08 07 06

CONTENTS

THE GREEKS, THEIR GODS, & MYTHS

The world of the ancient Greeks was bound by the Mediterranean Sea and the rugged lands surrounding it. It was a place of dangerous winds and sudden storms. The ancient Greeks saw their lives as controlled by spirits of nature and the gods. They told myths about how the gods fought with each other and created the universe. These stories helped explain what caused natural events, such as lightning and earthquakes, and the fates of individuals.

The ancient Greeks believed that 12 gods and goddesses ruled over the world. The 10 gods and goddesses shown on the next page are the most important ones. Some of them appear in this myth.

The ancient Greek gods and goddesses looked and acted like human beings. They fell in love, were jealous and vain, and argued with each other. But unlike humans, they were immortal. They did not die but lived forever. They also had superhuman strength and specific magical powers. Each god or goddess controlled certain forces of nature or aspects of human life, such as marriage or hunting.

In the myths, the gods had their favorite humans. Sometimes, the gods even had children with these people. Their children were thus half gods. They were usually mortal, which meant that they could die. It also meant that they had some special powers, too. When their human children were in trouble, the gods would help them.

The gods liked to meddle in human life and took sides with different people. The gods also liked to play tricks on humans. They did so for many reasons—because it was fun; because they would gain something; or because they wanted to get even with someone.

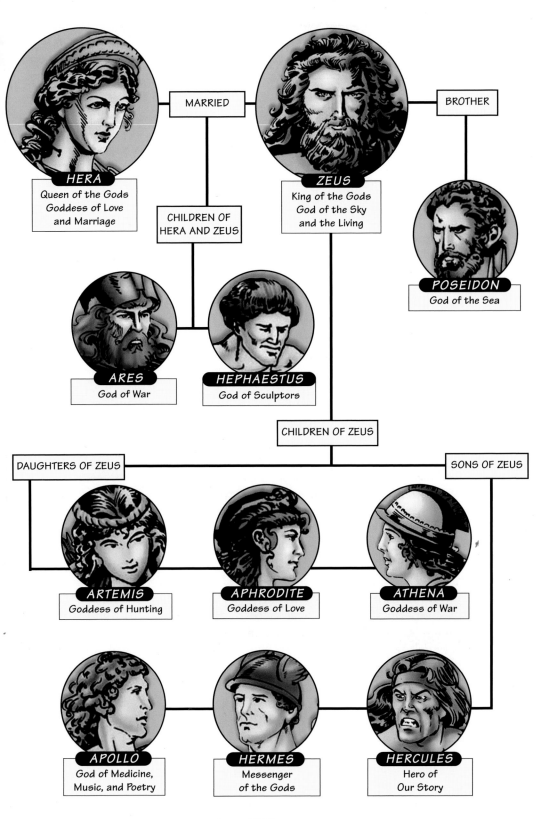

HERA — MARRIED — ZEUS — BROTHER

HERA
Queen of the Gods
Goddess of Love
and Marriage

ZEUS
King of the Gods
God of the Sky
and the Living

POSEIDON
God of the Sea

CHILDREN OF
HERA AND ZEUS

ARES
God of War

HEPHAESTUS
God of Sculptors

CHILDREN OF ZEUS

DAUGHTERS OF ZEUS

SONS OF ZEUS

ARTEMIS
Goddess of Hunting

APHRODITE
Goddess of Love

ATHENA
Goddess of War

APOLLO
God of Medicine,
Music, and Poetry

HERMES
Messenger
of the Gods

HERCULES
Hero of
Our Story

HOW THE MYTH BEGINS

The fate of the Greek hero Hercules certainly lay in the gods' hands. Zeus and Hera, the king and queen of the gods, had long argued over Zeus and his mortal women. Hera was jealous of the many children that Zeus had had with these humans. She hated his child Hercules most of all. Aided by other gods and goddesses, Hera tried to kill Hercules, first as a baby, then as a young man. But Hercules was strong and smart and managed to save himself many times. In addition, Zeus plotted against his wife and protected his son. Hercules' story shows that the gods could be cruel and kind—just like people.

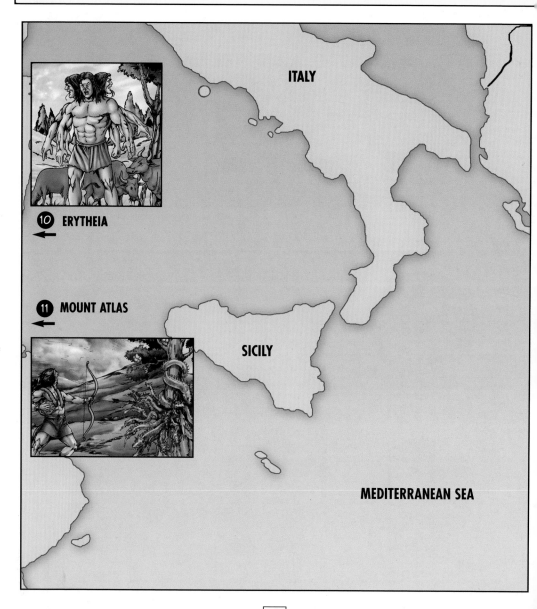

ITALY

🔟 ERYTHEIA

⓫ MOUNT ATLAS

SICILY

MEDITERRANEAN SEA

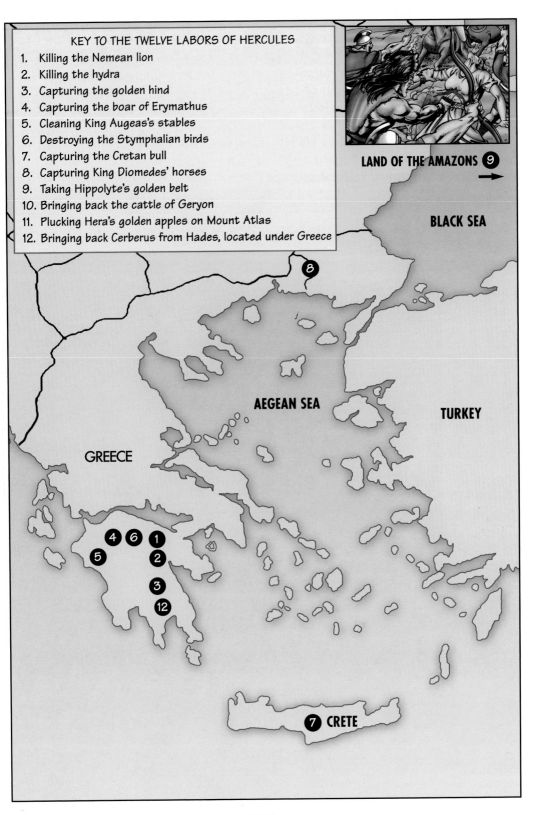

KEY TO THE TWELVE LABORS OF HERCULES

1. Killing the Nemean lion
2. Killing the hydra
3. Capturing the golden hind
4. Capturing the boar of Erymathus
5. Cleaning King Augeas's stables
6. Destroying the Stymphalian birds
7. Capturing the Cretan bull
8. Capturing King Diomedes' horses
9. Taking Hippolyte's golden belt
10. Bringing back the cattle of Geryon
11. Plucking Hera's golden apples on Mount Atlas
12. Bringing back Cerberus from Hades, located under Greece

LAND OF THE AMAZONS

BLACK SEA

AEGEAN SEA

TURKEY

GREECE

CRETE

BIRTH OF HERCULES

Although married, Zeus and Hera were always falling in love with other people. Of course, neither of them liked it when the other fell in love. Zeus's latest love was Alcmena, a wise and beautiful woman. But Alcmena wasn't interested in Zeus; she loved only her husband. But Zeus had other plans for her anyway. . . .

Alcmena didn't realize that the man in front of her was not her husband.

Full of anger, Hera sent two huge snakes to crush the baby Hercules while he slept in his crib.

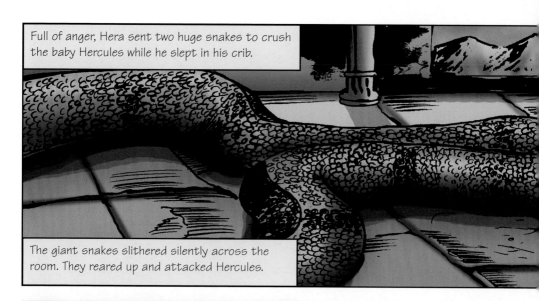

The giant snakes slithered silently across the room. They reared up and attacked Hercules.

Suddenly, Hercules jumped up. He grabbed the snakes and strangled them both.

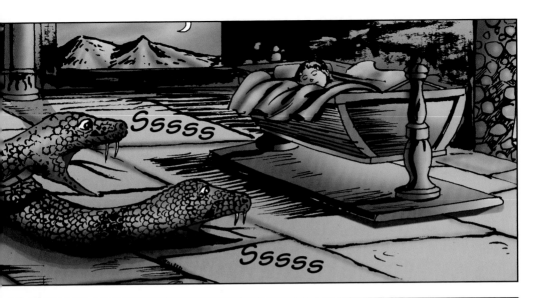

The next morning, servants entered the room. They were stunned at the sight. Two giant snakes lay dead on the floor. Baby Hercules was laughing and gurgling in his crib.

HERCULES' EARLY BATTLES

Hera had failed to kill Hercules as a child. That did not stop her from trying again and again as he grew up, however. Hercules was hard to kill. He had inherited amazing strength from his father, Zeus. Once Hera realized that she couldn't kill Hercules by herself, she asked other gods to help her. Many of the gods were jealous of Hercules' strength and agreed to help Hera. Zeus knew what Hera was planning. He asked other gods to help him protect Hercules.

One of Hercules' first battles was against Cyncus, the cruel son of the war god, Ares. He lived in Thessaly in northern Greece. Cyncus was building a temple to his father. He attacked pilgrims on their way to the temple, killed them, and stole their belongings. Their skulls became the building blocks of the temple to Ares. Hercules was passing the temple when Cyncus dared him to a fight. Their battle was over quickly. Hercules had won.

Next, Hercules fought Syleus, a cruel outlaw. Syleus grabbed passing strangers and forced them to work in his vineyards. When they finished their jobs, he murdered them. Hercules killed Syleus and brought an end to his reign of terror.

Syleus, you murderer! Now you will never kill innocent men again!

Aaaghhh!

Hercules was also strong enough to fight against armies of men. The Lapiths were a fierce tribe. Their name means "men of stone or flint." They were the enemies of the centaurs and fought many battles with these half-men, half-horse creatures. The centaurs asked Hercules to defeat the Lapiths. Hercules did in a huge, bloody fight. In thanks, the centaurs gave Hercules one-third of their kingdom.

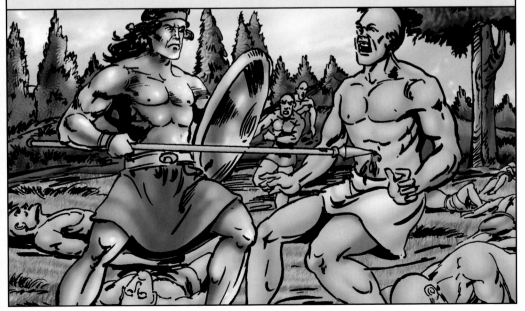

Hercules' next big battle was against the cruel King Erginus. A group of Greeks from the city of Thebes had killed King Erginus's father, Clymenus. In revenge, Erginus captured Thebes. He demanded a payment of 100 oxen each year for 20 years from its people. This injustice angered the goddess Athena. She knew Hercules was strong enough to fight Erginus, so she sent him to free Thebes. Hercules cleverly ambushed Erginus and defeated him.

The king of Thebes, Creon, was grateful to Hercules. When Hercules fell in love with Creon's daughter, the king happily gave his blessing to their marriage.

I am happy to be marrying such a wonderful man.

Hercules married Megara in a royal wedding at Thebes. They had three sons.

Hercules, look! What a handsome baby we have.

For a time, Hercules was very happy. But that changed when Pyraechmus, attacked Hercules' new home, Thebes. Pyraechmus was king of the Euboeans. He wanted to kill Hercules in revenge for the death of his friend Erginus.

Hercules easily beat the Euboeans. As punishment, he tied King Pyraechmus between two horses. Then Hercules watched as the horses tore the king's body in two. The people of Greece were horrified by this cruel act.

Pyraechmus, I want you to suffer.

Hercules then left Pyraechmus's body unburied on the banks of the river Heracleius. This was a terrible crime. The gods had ruled that everyone must be given a proper burial!

Hera was filled with rage at Pyraechmus's defeat. She cast a magic spell on Hercules.

Hercules has disobeyed our rules. None of the gods can disagree with me for punishing him for it.

By the gods! What is wrong with my head? I feel like it's going to explode.

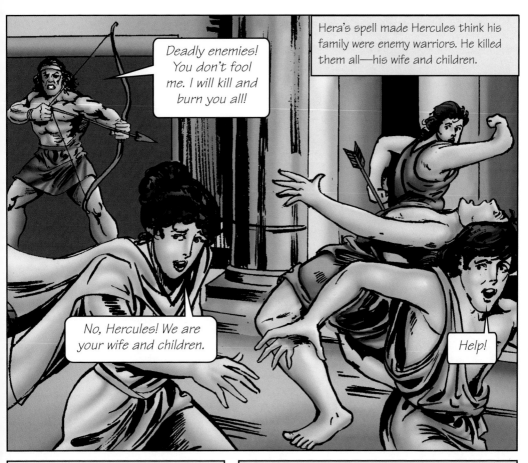

Hera's spell made Hercules think his family were enemy warriors. He killed them all—his wife and children.

Deadly enemies! You don't fool me. I will kill and burn you all!

No, Hercules! We are your wife and children.

Help!

When the madness wore off, Hercules instantly regretted his actions. Overcome by grief, he locked himself away to think about what to do next.

Oh Zeus what have I done? I cannot live with myself any longer.

Hercules decided to ask the gods for help. He went to see the oracle in Apollo's temple. Hercules asked her what he could do to make up for his awful crimes. He could not know that Hera herself controlled the oracle and influenced her words. . . .

You must be the slave of King Eurystheus for 12 years and do whatever he tells you to do. Then you shall be forgiven.

HERCULES' 12 LABORS

Hera had helped Eurystheus become king of Tiryns, an important land. Eurystheus thus agreed to do whatever Hera asked of him. Together they plotted to kill Hercules. They would assign him to dangerous tasks, tasks no one could complete—and live. There was supposed to be one labor for each of Hercules' 12 years of slavery—if he survived.

Wicked Hercules, you are in my power. I shall punish you with twelve labors. You must complete every one! If not . . .

He cannot survive these tasks. Each one could kill him.

Task 1

For Hercules' first task, King Eurystheus demanded that he kill the lion of Nemea. This beast constantly attacked the shepherds of Nemea. It was a huge, cruel creature with magical skin. No arrow or spear could pierce its thick hide.

Dearest wife, you have cursed my son Hercules. These twelve labors will make us fight against each other.

Hercules searched for the lion for a long time. He finally found the gloomy cave where it lived. He approached the entrance carefully, but the lion heard him. It jumped out, its claws and fangs bared. Hercules stunned the beast with his club and strangled it. He then used the lion's claws to cut off its skin.

Killer lion! You have met your match in me! Once I have killed you, I will wear your magical skin to protect me against weapons.

You cannot win, my lord. You shall see my true powers now! Hercules shall die!

From then on, whenever Hercules went into battle, he wore the lion's hide and head to protect himself from attack.

Task 2 For his second task, Hercules was sent to kill the nine-headed water snake—the Hydra. He was allowed to take his nephew, Iolaus, to help him. The monster was huge and fierce. Hercules tried to avoid its snapping jaws and attacked it with his sword and club.

I have made this monster, the Hydra, to finish Hercules off.

Hiss

Hiss

It seemed that this monster would be too much for the great Hercules. It wound itself around Hercules, trapping the hero in its slippery coils.

Hercules twisted free. But each time he sliced off one of the monster's heads, it grew another one. Hercules could not beat the Hydra by himself. He called to his nephew, Iolaus, for help. Between them, they came up with a brilliant plan.

I will, my lord!

Iolaus, faithful friend, use your fiery torch to burn the blood and stop a new head from growing!

Their plan worked! Eight heads lay on the ground, the ninth pinned beneath a rock. Hercules dipped his arrows in the Hydra's blood, tipping them with poison.

Hercules' next task was to capture a golden hind—alive. This young deer was special to the goddess Artemis. It was a beautiful animal with golden antlers and bronze hooves.

Hercules shall kill your special hind, daughter!

Oh powerful mother, if he does, he shall die by my arrow.

There! If I pin its legs to the tree, I can trap it without killing it or insulting Artemis.

Hercules carried the golden hind to King Eurystheus. The king wanted to keep it, but Hercules knew this would offend Artemis.

Once I let go, he'll never catch it.

Of course, I can catch such a small creature.

Here Eurystheus! I will let go of the hind. If you can catch it, you can keep it.

But the hind ran off before King Eurystheus could even touch it.

So far, Hercules had finished each task set for him. Even though Hera and Eurystheus made sure that each task was harder than the last, Hercules remained healthy and whole. Hera had misjudged Hercules' bravery, strength, and cleverness. She had also misjudged the power of her husband, Zeus. The god was helping Hercules whenever he could.

Task 4 For his fourth task, Hercules had to hunt down and capture a giant wild boar. It was attacking people in the countryside of Erymanthus.

Drunken centaurs attacked Hercules on his way to Erymanthus. He defended himself bravely, killing many of the centaurs with his poisoned arrows. Only one, called Nessus, escaped.

After the battle, Hercules continued his search for the boar. He found its tracks and followed them to the creature. When he had crept close to the huge beast, Hercules threw a large net over it. Then he tied the boar up, careful to avoid its sharp tusks.

Hercules took the beast back to Eurystheus. The king was indeed scared by it and had it taken away.

Task 5 The sea god Poseidon helped set Hercules' fifth task. He asked King Eurystheus to give Hercules the job of cleaning out the stables of his son, King Augeas. King Augeas kept a herd of 3,000 cattle and sheep. They lived in stables that had never been cleaned. Dung heaps covered the floor. King Eurystheus gave Hercules one day to do the work.

This will be fun to watch. I doubt that Hercules will be able to finish this task.

However, King Eurystheus had forgotten about Hercules' clever mind. In no time, Hercules completed his task by changing the direction of two rivers. They flowed down the valley, through the stable walls, and washed away all the filth. The stables were clean.

I've done it! Eurystheus won't be happy about this. He'll have to make the next task harder.

The war god, Ares, was angry with Hercules for killing his son. He offered to help Eurystheus and set Hercules' next task. Ares had a flock of birds called the Stymphalians. Their beaks, talons, and wings were made of iron. Their feathers were tipped with arrows. As their feathers fell to earth, they killed the birds' prey—humans. The Stymphalians then ate the humans or carried them away. King Eurystheus ordered Hercules to kill the birds.

Hercules can never defeat my Stymphalian birds. He is finished!

Zeus asked his daughter, the goddess Athena, to help.
Hercules found the stinking swamp where the birds lived.

My magic rattle is helping Hercules wake the birds.

Thanks to Athena, I'll soon get rid of you horrible creatures.

The startled birds flew up. Hercules then
shot each one with his bow and arrow. Ares
had misjudged Hercules' skills as an archer.

Terrible monsters, you have eaten your last human meal.

King Eurystheus then ordered Hercules to trap a fire-breathing bull. Poseidon had given the bull to King Minos of Crete to sacrifice it in the god's honor. Instead, the king kept the bull, so Poseidon drove the creature crazy. Now it was attacking the people of Crete.

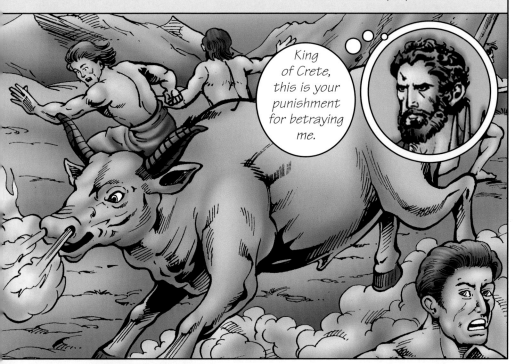

Hercules tracked the bull down and wrestled it to the ground. He carried the bull back and presented it to King Eurystheus.

TERRIBLE TASKS

King Eurystheus was a greedy man. He sent Hercules all over Greece to collect objects that he wanted. Some of these objects were riches, others were fantastic animals.

Task 8 King Diomedes was known throughout the lands of the Greeks for his cruelty. He also kept a herd of man-eating horses. For his eighth task, Hercules had to capture these fierce beasts.

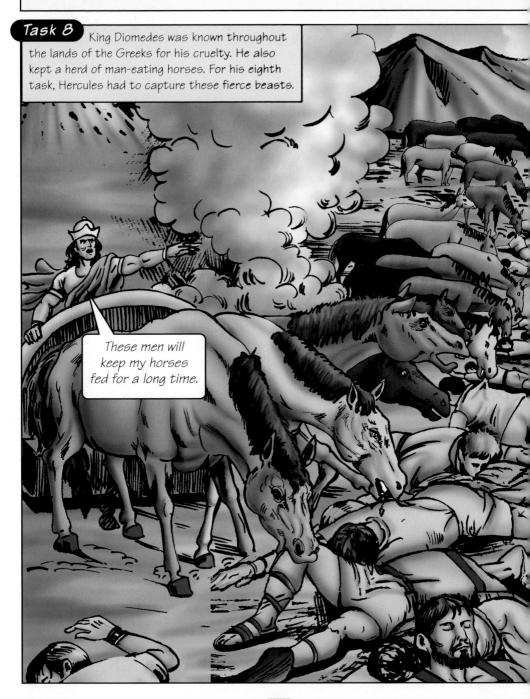

These men will keep my horses fed for a long time.

King Eurystheus sent Hercules to capture these horses for him. Diomedes didn't realize why Hercules was there.

Hello, King Diomedes.

Welcome Hercules, son of Zeus!

One night, Hercules rushed past the guards. He cut the horses' chains and set them free.

Stop! Thief!

The furious Diomedes and his guards chased Hercules. To stop them, Hercules carved a huge channel across the plain with his club. The plain flooded, drowning the men who had chased him.

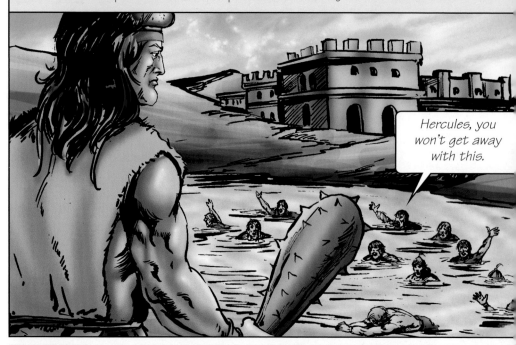

Hercules fed Diomedes' body to the wild horses. Strangely, they became tame and never ate human flesh again. Then Hercules took the whole herd back to Tiryns and gave them to King Eurystheus.

Task 9

Hercules' ninth task began when Princess Admete asked her father, King Eurystheus, for a favor. She wanted the golden belt worn by Hippolyte, queen of the Amazons.

Father, I want to wear the great golden belt of the Amazon Queen, Hippolyte.

I will send Hercules to get this belt for you.

Hercules will finish this task. You can't stop him now, Hera.

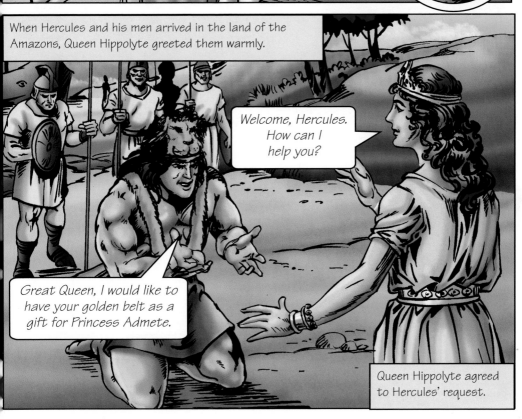

When Hercules and his men arrived in the land of the Amazons, Queen Hippolyte greeted them warmly.

Welcome, Hercules. How can I help you?

Great Queen, I would like to have your golden belt as a gift for Princess Admete.

Queen Hippolyte agreed to Hercules' request.

However, Hera was very angry that Hercules was about to finish another task. She disguised herself as an Amazon and spread stories that Hercules planned to kidnap Hippolyte.

Hippolyte's warriors were very angry and attacked Hercules. During the battle, Hercules killed Hippolyte and took her golden belt.

Yes, Amazons, it is true. Hercules will kidnap your queen unless you kill him first.

The gods have willed that Admete shall wear the golden belt. I have completed my task.

Hercules sailed back to Greece and presented the golden belt to Princess Admete.

Fed up with Hercules' successes, King Eurystheus set him a much harder task. In the land of Erytheia lived Geryon, a monster with three heads. He kept a herd of red cattle. King Eurystheus demanded that Hercules kill Geryon and bring the cattle back to Tiryns.

Hercules arrived at Erytheia and hurried on to fight Geryon. But before Hercueles even set eyes on Geryon, his man-eating dogs attacked him.

I have fought far worse monsters than you, two-headed beast.

As soon as Hercules had killed the dogs, Geryon's herdsman attacked him. The fight was short and bloody.

Geryon roared with anger when he saw what Hercules had done. He stomped slowly toward Hercules. Before he could attack, Hercules killed Geryon with one arrow. He rounded up the cattle and returned to King Eurystheus with them.

DEATH AND LIFE

Hercules was the strongest, most successful hero the gods had ever seen. The fact that he finished each task made Hera and Eurystheus angrier and angrier. Thus Hercules' last two tasks were the most dangerous of all. Eurystheus hoped they would finally lead to the hero's death.

Task 11 For his eleventh task, Eurystheus cleverly sent Hercules on a mission that would deeply upset Hera. The king ordered Hercules to steal Hera's wedding present, the golden apples of Hesperides. The king hoped that Hera would be so angry that she would stop Hercules. Hercules' first problem was getting to the tree. A huge 100-headed dragon called Ladon guarded it. Then he had to find a way to pick the apples from the tree. The only people who could pick the apples were the Hesperides, the daughters of the Titan, Atlas.

Atlas held up the heavens. Hercules offered to help Atlas if the Titan helped him. Atlas agreed, so Hercules took the heavens from him. In return, Atlas told his daughters to pick the golden apples for Hercules.

Atlas, I will hold the heavens while you order your daughters to pick the apples.

When they were finished, Atlas refused to take back the heavens. Then Hercules asked Atlas to hold the heavens for just a moment until he could get comfortable. Atlas agreed, but Hercules then escaped with the apples.

Atlas, my friend, I must leave you to your fate.

Task 12 King Eurystheus was furious when Hercules brought him the apples. He ordered the hero to bring him the three-headed dog, Cerberus. This horrifying dog guarded the Underworld. No mortal man had gone into the Underworld and come out again. Zeus sent the god Hermes to help Hercules. As soon as Hercules stepped into the Underworld, six evil and powerful women known as the Fates and Furies attacked him. They didn't want Hercules there. Using his strength and cleverness, Hercules escaped them.

This is Hercules' most dangerous mission. I will guide him through the Underworld.

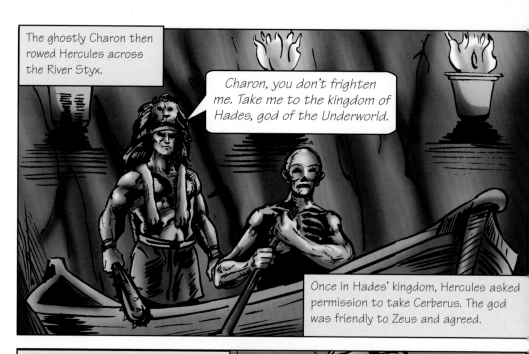

The ghostly Charon then rowed Hercules across the River Styx.

Charon, you don't frighten me. Take me to the kingdom of Hades, god of the Underworld.

Once in Hades' kingdom, Hercules asked permission to take Cerberus. The god was friendly to Zeus and agreed.

Cerberus was not willing to go, and no weapons worked against it. Hercules had to battle the three-headed monster with his bare hands.

You beasts are hard to fight, but I will defeat you.

Finally, Hercules flung a net over Cereberus, capturing it alive.

When Hercules took the huge dog to Eurystheus, the king ran away in terror.

Great king, you are defeated. Here is the horrible Cerberus. Now I have finished my twelve labors! I am free!

Finally Hercules was free. He left Tiryns to build a life for himself. Before long, Hercules had fallen in love and married a wonderful woman, Deianira.

It was the moment one of his old enemies, the centaur Nessus, had been waiting for. He attacked Deianira, determined to ruin Hercules' happiness. But the hero killed him.

Beautiful Deianira, I am free of the cruel Eurystheus at last. Will you marry me?

Before he died, Nessus had given Deianira drops of his blood. He promised her that it was a magical charm to keep Hercules in love with her. After some years, Deianira became worried that Hercules' love for her had fled. She put some of Nessus's blood onto Hercules' tunic. But the blood was poison. When Hercules put it on, the tunic burned his flesh.

Hercules is losing interest in me.

Aaargh

The dying Hercules was laid on a burning funeral pyre. But Zeus sent his magical thunderbolts to save him.

Hercules was taken from Earth on Zeus's chariot. The hero traveled to Mount Olympus, where Zeus made him immortal. Realizing that Hercules was not a threat to her, Hera finally forgave him. Hercules lived a very contented, peaceful life with the other gods.

GLOSSARY

Amazons *a mythical race of warrior women who lived without men in Scythia. Descended from the war god, Ares, they lived by hunting and were ruled by a queen.*

ambushed *attacked by surprise from a hidden position*

Apollo *the god of prophecy and music*

Atlas *a Titan whose name means "he who carries." In Greek myth, Atlas supported the sky.*

centaurs *a race of creatures with the head, arms, and upper body of a man and the lower body and legs of a horse*

Cerberus *a huge three-headed dog that guarded the Underworld. He ate those who tried to escape from Hades.*

Charon *a ghostly man who ferried the dead from the land of the living across the river Styx to the Underworld*

Crete *the largest of the Greek islands*

funeral pyre *a specially built bonfire on which the dead were laid and then burned as part of traditional Greek funeral rites.*

hind *a female deer, the golden hind was sacred to Artemis. Hercules hunted it for a year before capturing it.*

inherited *gained something from one's relatives*

Lapiths *legendary race of warriors from Thessaly in northern Greece*

mortal *able to die*

Mount Olympus *a snow-capped mountain in northern Greece. According to myths, it is the home of the gods.*

oracle *a person through whom a god or goddess is believed to speak. By consulting an oracle, the ancient Greeks believed they could discover the will of the gods.*

pilgrims *people who travel to a holy place to worship*

revenge *to get even for something done wrong to a person*

sacrifice *an offering, such as a specially killed animal, to a god in the hope of winning the god's support*

Titan *a member of a race of gods who ruled the world before Zeus and his gods. They were giant creatures, the children of Uranus (Sky) and Gaia (Earth).*

Underworld *in ancient Greek myths, where the dead exist, under the earth*

BOOKS

Burleigh, Robert. *Hercules*. New York: Steck-Vaughn, 1999.

Ford, James Evelyn. *The Twelve Labors of Hercules*. Ancient Myths (series). Minneapolis: Picture Window Books, 2004.

Galloway, Priscilla. *My Hero, Hercules*. Tales of Ancient Lands (series). Toronto: Annick Press, 1999.

McCaughrean, Geraldine. *Hercules*. Heroes (series). Peterborough, NH: Cricket Books, 2005.

Richardson, Adele. *Hercules*. World Mythology and Folklore (series). Mankato, MN: Capstone Press, 2003.

WEB SITES

Hercules for Kids
people.uncw.edu/deagona/herakles/children/home.htm
Background on Hercules including maps and information on how the gods are related plus Hercules' twelve labors

Hercules—Greece's Greatest Hero
www.perseus.tufts.edu/Herakles
Everything you wanted to know abut Hercules, illustrated with photos of Greek pottery that tell his tale

Hercules—History for Kids
www.historyforkids.org/learn/greeks/religion/myths/herakles.htm
What Hercules meant to the Greek people

Hercules: The Labors of Heracles from Greek Mythology
www.mythweb.com/hercules/index.htm
Cartoon figures illustrate the twelve labors of Hercules

Publisher's note to educators and parents: Our editors have carefully reviewed these Web sites to ensure that they are suitable for children. Many Web sites change frequently, however, and we cannot guarantee that a site's future contents will continue to meet our high standards of quality and educational value. Be advised that children should be closely supervised whenever they access the Internet.

INDEX